Honest Hour

by Victoria Sviggum

Dedicated to:

my baby girl♡

Honest Hour was first performed at the Union Theatre on 26 July 2023 as part of Troupe 22 production *Fragmented* Mirror with the following cast:

Kat Abbey Devoy
Izzy Jennifer Adams
Fi Rachel Elizabeth Smith
Becks Jade Sophia Vertannes
Flo Estel Dima

Directed by Victoria Sviggum

Fragmented Mirror was produced by Abbey Devoy, Bethanie Hayes and Francesca Woods.

CHARACTERS:

A group of friends who met at university in London. They have since graduated and are now in their mid-to-late twenties working and still living in London.

Kat

Type A personality. A planner. "Mother" of the friends circle. (Is wearing something green)

Izzy

Kat's flat mate. Relaxed, "go with the flow" sort of vibe. Loves partying. Currently hungover.

Fi

Artistic, intellectual. Quick-witted with a sarcastic sense of humour. Lesbian.

Becks

Hopeless romantic. Driven by aesthetics, some might say superficial. Trying to become an influencer. (Is wearing something heart-themed)

Flo

Spiritual. Into astrology, signs and synchronicities. Trying to live a more eco-friendly and "natural" life.

SCENE:

Living room of KAT and IZZY's flat in London. There is a sofa and various mismatched seating around a coffee table. The kitchen is accessed by exiting stage right. IZZY, FI and BECKS are sitting around the coffee table with glasses of rosé.

KAT enters from stage right with a plate of mixed healthy finger foods (carrots, lettuce cups, hummus etc)

KAT

Ok, I know the plan is takeaway, but I thought a few "hors d'oeuvres" wouldn't go amiss! Don't worry Iz, don't get up, no help needed.

IZZY

Oh good. Yeah, didn't want to step on your independent woman vibes and all that.

KAT

Mmhmm.

BECKS

These look delish! You've even arranged the lettuce cups in the shape of hearts!

BECKS takes a photo with her phone.

FI

Ick.

BECKS
Well we are celebrating Valentine's Day after all!

FI
We're not celebrating. We're assembling in *protest* against a commercialised holiday created purely for the financial gain of already large-pocketed companies that benefit off making people feel like their love isn't legitimate unless they receive cards, chocolates, balloons, an expensive dinner,/

IZZY
/ A shag.

FI (cont.)
all on this one arbitrary date in February.

BECKS
Geez, romantic much?

FI
Blind consumerist much? Nice outfit.

IZZY
Oh the gloves are off!

BECKS
Sorry for enjoying life and being excited
at the prospect of celebrating love.
We can't all be grumpy grinches like you.

FI

Yes, I'm sure the extra amount of independent thinking you'd have to do would wreak "absolute havoc" on your skin!

BECKS

Believe me, if I had any prospects, I'd definitely be out at a romantic restaurant with a muscly man, not getting take-out with your charming arse.

FI

"Takeout"? What are you American?

KAT

Now now you two, the night is still so young. Do you think we can leave intellectual squabbles until dessert?

FI

Intellectual, debateable.

IZZY

Ah no fun!

FI & BECKS

She started it.

KAT

And I'm ending it. Look we're all here together, first time in ages; celebrating, not Valentine's Day but Galentine's Day! Which can both be seen as a protest of the original holiday or a happy nod. Alright? Alright.

IZZY
Has anyone heard from Flo by the way?
She texted the chat?

Fi
Not since the cryptic emoji sequence: evil eye,
weighing scales, telescope and ferris wheel,
whatever that means.

BECKS
I think it's nice she uses the not-so-common emojis.
I imagine it makes them feels more popular.

FI
Yeah, 'cause usually the telescope just cries and
eats lunch by itself because the other emojis
won't sit with it.

IZZY
What the actual f-/

KAT
/Well, we may as well decide on where to order from
while we wait. Any suggestions?

FI
Vegetarian for me.

BECKS
Gluten-free for me.

IZZY

I'm up for anything, except kebab (makes face); I had a pretty regrettable experience with one last night.

KAT

Well, me too pretty much. Not the kebab bit, but up for anything. I'd love to try something new though, not just bog-standard pizza.

IZZY

Makes sense.

KAT

So how about Chinese, there's that new,-

BECKS

Mm, too oily.

KAT

Ok, Indian, they've got a great sele-

FI

Too spicey.

KAT

Turkish then?

IZZY

(gags) Too reminiscent of kebab...

KAT

(getting irritated) Thai?

FI

Had that last night.

KAT

Sushi.

BECKS

Too spenny.

KAT

Greek!?

IZZY

(gags) Too reminiscent of kebab!!

KAT

(defeated with slight pause)...So what about pizza?

BECKS

Giuseppe's does a gluten-free base!

FI

Loads of veggie options.

IZZY

Makes sense.

KAT

Fine. Giuseppe's it is.

BECKS
Ooh yay! Thank God it's cheat day.

FI
(sarcastic) Thank the absolute heavens!

KAT
But we can't order until Flo gets here. Still nothing?

IZZY
Snooze you lose I say.

KAT
She's not snoozing, she's probably just, -

FI
She probably saw a random cat,
deemed it lucky and followed it around for a bit...

BECKS
What, that's crazy!

KAT
Yes...that only happened once.

BECKS
What, actually?

IZZY
Yeah, Flo is, what they call "in tune"
with the universe now...

FI
In tune with something, that's for sure.

KAT
Be nice.

BECKS
She's a Pisces right?
They do tend to be more psychic.

FI
Oh my god, the disease is spreading.

IZZY
I'm staaarrrrvvvving!

KAT
Look we'll give her ten more minutes. You can have a carrot and some hummus in the mean time.

IZZY
Gee thanks mum. Did I mention I was *hungover*?

KAT
I warned you not to mix drinks.

IZZY
Where's your sense of adventure?

KAT
Nicely positioned next to my sense of reality
and acceptance that we can no longer

drink like teenagers.

BECKS
It's true. Too much alcohol, is so bad for your skin.

FI
And the braincells.

KAT
And overall decision making.

[long pause]

IZZY
Anyone want more wine?

KAT/BECKS/FI
Oooh yes. / Me please! / Good idea.

KAT
There's another bottle of rosé in the fridge.

IZZY gets up to get the wine, exits stage right.

KAT (cont.)
Speaking of, I bumped into Rose yesterday.

BECKS
Ah Rose! How is she?
Haven't seen her properly since uni!

FI
Was she the girl with cute freckles,
amazing eyes, bum shaped like a peach?

BECKS
Calm your tits.

FI
What? Just want to make sure
I have the right visual in mind.

KAT
Um, she may have had freckles yes.
She was in our classics class.

FI
Yup, got the right visual.

BECKS
Perv.

KAT
Well, and now I'm not usually one to gossip,-

IZZY
(off-stage) Ha!

KAT
Honestly, it's a very unladylike trait.

FI
'Unladylike'?

IZZY enters with rosé.

IZZY

Well good thing for us, and Arun,
that you're not a lady ey?

KAT

Excuse me, I –

BECKS

What's the goss?!

IZZY

Yeah, we know you're gagging to tell us.

KAT

Fine. So you know how Rose and Dan got married?
Well she just found out he's gay –
walked in on him in a very compromising
position with one of his "mates".

KAT is looking for a reaction and is not getting much.

KAT (cont.)

Can you imagine? After three years of marriage!?

IZZY

Lame.

FI

Bit disappointing.

BECKS
Old news.

KAT
What?

IZZY
Everyone knows Danny's gay.

FI
Yeah, doesn't take a queer
to recognise *that* queer.

KAT
You're joking, you all knew?

BECKS
I thought *she* knew.

IZZY
Yeah like they had come to some sort of jammy
agreement. Shag who you like behind closed doors,
but be the perfect couple in public.

FI
Yeah, common knowledge, everyone knew.

KAT
Well I have a mascara-soaked scarf that confirms
Rose definitely did *not* know.
She was a complete shambles, crying about
moving back in with her parents.

IZZY
Well I'd be crying too if I had to move to Slough.

BECKS
I thought she was from Milton Keynes?

IZZY
Somewhere like that. Not London that's for sure.

FI
I might need to consider extending
my catchment area on Hinge...

KAT
Guys! Are you seriously telling me you all knew?

BECKS
Well, yeah.

KAT
This girl, who at some point, we were friends with,
wasted, what, five years of her life with someone
she thought would love her to "death do her part"?

IZZY
Enter the drama.

KAT
No I'm sorry, but this is so depressing!

BECKS
Well no one says he didn't love her.

FI
Why are you getting so bent out of shape?

KAT
Her whole relationship was a lie!
And apparently everyone knew!
I mean why didn't you tell her?

IZZY
Hey that's not fair.

BECKS
Yeah, it's not like we were her close friends.

FI
Exactly! Though I'm pretty sure they knew too.

KAT
I don't believe this. Her life, ruined
because no one was honest with her.

IZZY
Well why didn't *you* tell her?!

KAT
I didn't know!

FI
Yeah, you do take people at face value.

One of your more naïve,
yet strangely attractive traits.

KAT
I mean, is there something you're not telling me?
Is Arun gay? He did love it when I had that pixie cut...

BECKS
Oooh yeah, that was not your best look./
Wrong face shape.

IZZY
/Oh my god Kat, you need to calm down.

KAT
I'm sorry, I just can't. This is mind boggling to me.
I mean, she thought she had friends
and not *one* told her. I mean, we're women,
we should be helping and supporting each other,

FI
Here, here.

KAT
Not lying to each other;
we owe each other more than that.

IZZY
Please can we eat first,
before you go on a feminist rant!

FI
Let her continue, she looks so cute on her soap box.

BECKS
Actually, my blood sugar's getting kind of low so,-

KAT
I'm serious guys, I want us to be honest with each other. I don't want to be happily plodding along with my life to only one day be smacked in the face with a fact that could ruin everything!
I have a five-year plan in place for God's sake.

IZZY
Did you hear that?
I think my stomach actually screamed.

KAT
Ok, look, I'll order the bloody pizza now if you all agree to be unapologetically honest and tell me something I may not be aware of.

BECKS
What?

KAT
A truth about me, that you know, that I may not!

BECKS tries to work out the sentence in her head.

IZZY

(sighs) Promise? And then we order?

KAT

Promise.

IZZY

(looking to the others in defeat)
I'm not loving those boots.

BECKS

Green was never your colour.

BECKS and IZZY gesture to FI.

FI

Oh...ummm...your handwriting is not great.

KAT

That's it?

FI

Well actually / more often that not it's illegible.

BECKS

/ It's just not your colour season.

KAT

Well thank you for your candidness but I was looking for something a bit more meaningful, less superficial. You know something *life-changing*.

BECKS
Learning your colours can totally change your world.
My money's on bright winter!

IZZY
(irritated) Look you promised we would order the pizza, so unless you want to add "doesn't keep promises" to that list, Deliveroo is a-calling!

KAT
(sigh) Fine. Meat Feast for you I take it?

IZZY
With extra cheese and jalapeños!

FI
Veggie supreme for me!

BECKS
And gluten-free margherita for me.

KAT
Hawaii for me...

IZZY
You want a truth?
Pineapple on pizza should be illegal
and the people who like it locked up.

KAT
What do you think Flo will want?

FLO
[off-stage] She wants a hug!

FLO enters upstage right.

FLO (cont.)
Hi girls, so sorry I'm late, I got on the wrong bus.

IZZY
(to KAT) Did you order?!

KAT
That's odd, you've been here loads.

IZZY
Confirm, did you press *confirm*?

FLO
Oh yes, I know, it's just the 333 pulled up to the
bus stop at exactly thirty-three past,
so, well I had no choice but to get on right?

FI
Well of course not.

KAT
So you took the wrong bus on purpose?

IZZY
Click, have you clicked?

FLO

Angel numbers have been calling to me lately.
111, 222, -

FI

666?

FLO

Make fun all you want but it's the universe
sending signals. Every time I've followed them,
they lead me to something magical.

IZZY

Flo, you want vegan right?
Kat, can you add that to the order and submit?

BECKS

Wow, so what did the bus lead you too?
A very rich, very handsome man?

FLO

(slight laughter) Oh no, my guides know that I need to
protect my feminine energy right now.
Nourish and get to know myself you know?
So not allowing any men
into my sphere at the moment.

BECKS

(sighs) I wish I had a man in my sphere.

FI

Kinky.

BECKS
Ew, I didn't mean it like that!

KAT
So what did the bus lead you to?

FI
Yes, we're all *dying* to know.

IZZY
Kat, the pizza? The pizza Kat!

FLO
Organic kitty litter.

FI
Come again?

FLO
The route took us passed this darling little pet shop
advertising eco-friendly kitty litter.
I've been looking for it for quite some time;
you know Grumbles loves the planet
and wants to give back.
I couldn't believe it, the stars just aligned!

FLO removes her scarf, pops down bag.

FI
So you're almost 45 minutes late, so your cat
can defecate in a more environmentally-friendly
way?...Makes sense.

Awkward pause.

BECKS
Does it at least come in a cute colour?

KAT
Well I think it's great! We really need everyone to get stuck in when it comes to preserving the planet.

IZZY
I don't think I can feel my face.

KAT
Then you should stop drinking. Right let's order. Vegan pizza for you Flo?

FLO
We always get pizza. We should try something else.

(everyone except KAT lets out an exasperated moan)

KAT
Unfortunately we've already been round the block on this one. Pizza seems to be the least problematic.

FLO
Ok well that's fine, I'll just go with the majority. Vegan for me!

KAT
Great, ok, (taps phone) oh no...error message.

IZZY
Oh...my...God.

KAT
Would you like to order Iz?
We can stick it on your card?

IZZY
(like a scolded child) It's fine, I can wait.

KAT
That's what I thought, it'll be up and running
in a sec I'm sure.

FLO
So what is with the energy in the room?
It feels very...(using hands) static-y.

FI
Well Izzy's hungover and starving.
Becks is missing the D and Kat tried to change our
girls' night into Honest Hour with Dr. Phil.

BECKS
"Dr. Phil"? What are you American?

FI
(impressed) Touché.

FLO
Honest Hour? That sounds interesting! Tell me more.

IZZY
Ugh, there's nothing to tell.

FLO looks expectant.

IZZY (cont.)
Kat bumped into Rose from Uni,

FLO
Rose? Oh, was she the girl in our classics module?

FI
Ass like a peach.

IZZY
Yes, Rose. Anyways, apparently she's getting divorced because she found out her long-term boyfriend-come-husband swings the other way.

FLO
Who did she go out with again?

BECKS
Danny, you remember Danny....Aquarius.

FLO
Oh of course. Everyone knew he was gay though didn't they?

IZZY
Exactly! Well apparently not Rose, or Kat,

who was so shocked and appalled that her friends had kept this secret from her for so long.
(speeds up) Anyway, she then proceeds to hold our pizza hostage until we all tell her a "truth" so she doesn't fuck up her five-year plan.
Becks thinks she is ugly in green, Fi said she writes like a psychopath and I told her those boots need the boot, now can we please order!!

KAT
Alright, alright, calm down.
App's up and running again.

IZZY
Yes!

FLO
Well I think that's a great idea.

FI
Great idea, debateable.

FLO
Yes, I mean the truth is the path to enlightenment.
Plus my therapist swears by it.

FI
Swears by what? The truth?

FLO
If she does group therapy, she'll ask everyone to

write something down about the other people that they find too hard to say in person.
It's all anonymous, so obviously doesn't work for couples, but we're five so it'd be perfect!

BECKS

Perfect?

FI

Does nobody else see the potential flaws in this idea?

KAT

I think it sounds fantastic!
I mean we might as well while we wait for the pizza right?

IZZY

So you *did* order, thank fu-

KAT

I'll get pens and paper!

KAT exits stage right.

BECKS

Guys, if I knew this was going to be some kind of brain storming evening, I would have,-

FI

Would have what? I thought you didn't have any other 'prospects'.

BECKS
Did I ever tell you I hate you?

FI blows her a kiss.
KAT enters with pens and pink flash cards.

KAT
Come on, it will be fun! And like Flo said, enlightening. Before you know it, you'll be munching on your gluten-free slice. I promise to let it go after.

IZZY
Your promises mean nothing!...
But if we're going to do this, we need more wine.

FLO
Oh yes, I brought some organic red!

FI
Did you know wine's not vegan?

FLO
What?

FI
Yeah, too many insects get killed in the process.

FLO
(very upset) Really?

BECKS
(interjecting) She's just messing with you Flo.

FI

...Yeah of course. Just joking.

FLO

(relieved) You. You're so cheeky sometimes, typical Gemini. I'll go open the bottle.

FI supresses a reaction to being called a typical Gemini.

KAT

I'll come with you, our bottle opener can be a bit tricky.

FLO and KAT exit stage right.

FI

Guys, is this really a good idea?
I mean, I'm no detective,
but people are bound to get upset.

BECKS

(unsure) It might be fun? I guess we could all do with a bit of constructive criticism now and then.

FI

You've changed your tune.

BECKS

Well, the cards are pink!

IZZY

Recipe for disaster I think, but you know what Kat's like when she has an idea. Dog with a bone.

FLO and KAT enter with bottle of wine.

KAT

Ok, how is this going to work...
everyone pass around the cards, four each.
One card per person. It's all anonymous.

FLO

And remember, this is a safe space.

IZZY

How are we going to keep it anonymous,
you'll be able to tell by our handwriting.

FI

Especially Kat's.

KAT

Well...try and write in a neutral style.

BECKS

Or someone else can read on behalf of another
so they don't see the cards themselves.

A moment of silence while everyone is stunned by BECK's logic.

FI
Exactly, so the person under fire
never sees what's written.

FLO
We're sharing enlightening truths,
not putting people *"under fire"*.
Remember we're creating a positive space.

IZZY
Or we could end up hating each other.

KAT
We won't, it'll probably make us closer!
Look, if it makes you feel any better,
we'll have a rule that nobody can get upset
at someone for sharing their truth.

FI
Fair.

KAT
Oh, and it can't be superficial, it has to be meaningful.
Ok everyone got a pen?

FLO
Kat, if I may, I'd like to set some
intentions for this session.

FI
Session?

KAT
Oh, absolutely.
(gestures to Flo that the floor is hers)

FLO
Everyone close their eyes.

IZZY
What?

KAT
The sooner you comply, the sooner we'll be done.

FLO
Let's take a few deep breaths together...

Everyone takes a few deep breaths with FLO leading. Different characters responding in different ways.

FLO (cont.)
We're inviting the truth into our lives so that it may enlighten and heal us. We go into this with love and positive energy so that it may be a safe space. Namaste.

IZZY
I am not getting into a downward dog.

FI
That's what she said.

FLO
Ok, our intention is set, we can begin.

BECKS
So, we just, one truth per person?

KAT
Yup!

BECKS
Ok.

Pause. They are all thinking. KAT goes to write something, then decides not to. FI does the same. Becks taps her pen.

FI
It's actually quite hard isn't it.

FLO
Don't force it, it'll come to you.

IZZY
As long as the pizza is coming to *us*!

KAT
Shh!

BECKS
And when you say "meaningful", you mean,

KAT
Something that would make a big difference to know.

BECKS
I still stand by the colour season thing, but ok...

Still no one writes anything.

IZZY
This is pointless. Has anyone written anything?

KAT
Maybe we just need some prompts.

BECKS
Like?

KAT
Like, I don't know, complete the following sentence:
"Kat would be better off if she knew [blank]" or
"If Izzy knew [blank] it would help her
make better decisions..."

IZZY
You don't think I make good decisions?

KAT
It was an example.

IZZY
Just funny that you chose me for that example.

KAT
Iz,

IZZY
What's the status on the pizza?

KAT
You're actually like a child. Probably cooking, so we all better get our skates on!

BECKS
Maybe set a timer? I work better under pressure.

FI
I can do it on my phone, two minutes?

BECKS
Two?!

FI
30 seconds per truth. Less time to think, just go with your gut.

FLO
I don't think this is something to be rushed.

KAT
Yeah, I -

FI
Go!

BECKS
Goodness!

Everybody starts writing.

BECKS
(panicking) Pen's not working, my pen's not working!

IZZY
Think fast!

IZZY chucks a pen at BECKS.

FI
Tick tock on the clock guys.

BECKS
Shut up, shut up, shut up!

IZZY
I still can't think of anything,
everyone's grand. I give up.

KAT
Typical.

IZZY
What does that mean?

KAT
Why are you always like this?
Why can't you get on board, and t*ry* for once.

FI
Half way!

BECKS
Shit, shit, shit.

FLO
Can you tell me when it's 1min11sec?

BECKS
Shit, shit, shit.

IZZY
Are you saying I never try?

FI
111 on the clock!

KAT
Shut up Izzy, I'm trying to write.

IZZY
No, I wanna know what you mean!

KAT
Maybe I'll write it down for you. Just write!

BECKS
Shit, shit, shit!

IZZY

Fine! Maybe I'll write something too!

KAT

Kind of the point.

FI

Ten seconds... 3, 2, 1, time!

BECKS

That was more stressful than post-Christmas sales!

FLO

I was reluctant at first, but once I opened my heart, it just poured out.

FI is still writing.

KAT

Fab! Fi, what you doing?

FI

Just finishing mine, was too focused on being the timekeeper- you're welcome by the way. Just one sec.

KAT

Well your efficiency is much appreciated.

BECKS

How nice for you don't have someone barking the seconds in your ear.

FI
No need to be sour sunshine, all done!

KAT
Ok, (pause) so I guess we pass them around?

FLO
I'll read Kat's.

KAT
I'll take Becks.

IZZY
Fi for me!

FI
I'll go with Flo.

BECKS
I guess that leaves me with Izzy.

KAT
Ok, pass the cards to the right person,
don't look at them yet!
And remember to shuffle!

There is an improvised kerfuffle as the cards are passed around.

BECKS
Is anyone else nervous? I'm glowing.

FI
Do you mean sweating?

BECKS
Girls glow, boys sweat.

FI
Ah, and non-binary people?

BECKS
Uh well I guess they can choose.

FI
How wonderful for them.

KAT
Ok, so who wants to go first?

FLO
Why don't we all read one each?

KAT
Good idea. Everyone look at their cards...now!

Everyone reads their cards and reacts individually.

FI
Well this just got interesting.

FLO
You know maybe it's not the right time for this.
Mercury is in retrograde and,-

BECKS
Yeah, maybe this wasn't such a good idea.

IZZY
No, no! *Kat* wanted to do this so let's do it!

KAT
Well...aren't you curious what's been said about you? We can start with the light ones and work our way up. Flo?

FLO
Um ok...well I guess...I'll start with...um...

IZZY
Just pick.

FLO
Ok. "Kat should know that she can't plan everything and she'd enjoy life more if she lived in the moment more."

KAT
Ok! That wasn't so bad! And yes, that's true, I do need to let go more, and,-

FLO (cont.)
"Her constant need for control can be a little annoying and can sometimes suck the fun out of group activities."

KAT

Oh...Ok, well...I mean my planning is to make group activities run smoother so everyone has a *better* time, but well I guess, that's just not appreciated.

IZZY

Ah ah aah. No getting upset remember?

KAT

(tries to compose herself) Yes, you're right...
ok, I'll take it on board.
Plan less, live in the moment more...
I'll put reminders in my calendar. Who's next? Becks?

BECKS

Um, I, -

KAT

Read Becks!

BECKS

Ok. So I have Izzy. "Izzy drinks too much."

IZZY

Guilty as charged. (Takes a sip of wine)

BECKS (cont.)

"Sometimes when we go out, people make bets on how long it will be before she voms."

IZZY

Fine by me.

I don't mind being a source of entertainment.
(Takes another gulp) Next!

FI

Ok, I guess I'll go. Ms Florence.
"Flo would make better decisions,
if she realised the "spiritual industry" is complete bullshit and the only thing it "manifests" is more money for the multi-million dollar companies pedalling that crap.

FLO

Ok, thanks Fi for your opinion,

FI

Who said it was me?

FLO

But I don't expect you to understand.
You're simply not quite as awakened.

FI

Awake enough to know a crystal
isn't going to solve all my problems.

FLO

Of course not, that would be ridiculous.
Different crystals have *different* healing properties.
You might benefit from rose quartz,

FI

Somebody punch me.

KAT

Ok, Ok, I'll go next. Becks, "Becks would be more successful if she focused her energy on a marketing career rather than Instagram."
That's not bad right? Sound advice.

BECKS

Who says I'm not successful?

IZZY

Um, anonymous, remember?

FI

I think she was being rhetorical.

FLO

But a good point. Success is something we must all define for ourselves.

BECKS

(defensive) Exactly. And I'm getting more followers every day. It's a grind. Nothing happens overnight.

KAT

Ok, ok. Shall we move on? Who hasn't been yet?

IZZY

Me with Fi.

FI

Let her rip.

IZZY
"Fi is a legend- no complaints.
Except she still owes me a tenner in cab fare."

FI
Fair.

KAT
I knew you wouldn't take this seriously.

IZZY
Loosen up Kat. "Be in the moment more."

KAT visibly annoyed.

IZZY (cont.)
I'm sure there are loads of goodies to come.
Time for another round?

KAT
Absolutely.

FLO
Ok, Kat, this person writes "As you are a Capricorn and
Arun is an Aries, you might consider seeking
a different partner like a Cancer or fellow earth sign
to avoid such an inflamed relationship."

IZZY
Some of these are a bit obvious guys.

BECKS
That's totally Flo!

FI
No shit Sherlock.

KAT
Thanks Flo. I'll take that into consideration.
Though maybe Arun and I are a zodiac exception.

IZZY
(wanting to stir)
Wonder what she meant by 'inflamed'...

KAT
Oh yes. That was quite an odd word to us.
What did you mean by that?

FLO
Oh, you know...Aries is a fire sign
and you're earth so...

FI
Basically kindling isn't it.

KAT
Oh, (slight laugh), sure I understand.

IZZY
Well alrighty then, let's move it along.
Fi, your next one is "Fi should know
that just because she only has sex with girls,

doesn't mean she doesn't need to use protection. She should get checked for STDs."

FI

(sarcastic) So *that's* what I missed in sex ed that day I skived off to snog Maddie behind the bins. Consider me LGBTQ clued up!

KAT

Fantastic. I hope everyone of us is practicing safe sex.

IZZY

(menacing) You'd hope so!

BECKS

Did you know you can get glow-in-the dark condoms? They're really fun!

FI

Are the men you sleep up with so clueless that they can't find their way around?

BECKS

Ha ha ha funny.

IZZY

I was amused.

KAT

Ok, I've got another one for Becks.

BECKS
(Takes a deep breath) Ok.

KAT
"Becks needs to ditch the fast fashion she buys for her YouTube channel. It contributes to child labour, pollutes the environment and is putting ethical manufacturers out of business."

BECKS
Sure you don't want to blame me for world hunger too?

FI
(impressed) That was a good one Becks.

BECKS
Shut up, it was you who wrote this.

FI
Actually it wasn't.

IZZY
A-NON-Y-MOUS!

KAT
Yes, please let's stick to the rules.
You can read your next one for Izzy.

BECKS
Fine. "If Izzy cut out dairy,
it might clear up her back acne."

IZZY
Back acne?

KAT
Ok, swiftly moving on!

IZZY
I have back acne?
(starts awkwardly trying to look over her shoulder)

BECKS
Can we stop? This isn't fun.

KAT
It's not supposed to be fun,
it's supposed to be insightful.

IZZY
Yes, God forbid we should be having
fun on a Friday night.
Is the food almost here yet?

KAT
Look, we're so close to finishing!

FI
I don't even think we're half way.

KAT
Give me another Flo!

FLO

Ok. "Kat is a bit of a control freak and can be too bossy. It's actually why," (starts squinting at card)

IZZY

Oooh, "controlling", that's two for two isn't it?

KAT

It's actually why what?

FLO

It looks like that bit was crossed out.

KAT

Huh. Well that's actually a shame, because alone, that's really quite vague. It would actually be better to have concrete examples.

IZZY

Well, (gestures with hand) Exhibit A: enforced therapy on Galentine's Day.

KAT

Ok ok, anything else though?
Please guys this would honestly help me.
I can take it.

FI

Well...you know you love a good schedule for, well everything...nights out,-

BECKS
Birthdays,

FLO
Glastonbury,

IZZY
Bathroom breaks,

FI (cont.)
With strict timings and everything.
It's sometimes a bit...much.

KAT
Does everyone feel this way?
I'm just trying to maximise the fun time.

IZZY
Maximise glum time more like.

FLO
Well Kat, what I think we're, or rather that person is saying is, that everyone would have a bett- more relaxed time if you laid off the planning just a bit.

FI
Nobody's saying you're not fun Kat!

BECKS
Yeah, just not, woah, crazy wild, Ibiza-style fun!

KAT
(reacting to Ibiza) What?

BECKS covers her mouth realising she's let something slip.

BECKS
What? Nothing. It was just a saying.

KAT
"Ibiza-style fun" is a saying?

FI
Yeah you know, like
"Spring break, woo hoo, get your tits out!"

KAT has a moment of realisation.

KAT
Is this why you went to Ibiza without me?

Awkward silence.

KAT (cont.)
Why you booked it during my probation
at my new job?

FLO
No, no, we told you, it was the only dates that would work for that amazing deal with the villa and...

IZZY
Yeah, too good of a deal to turn down...

BECKS
It was a limited offer!

Everyone looks to FI to back them up.

FI
Oh, yeah, basically 90% off.

Pause.

KAT
I don't believe this. Ditched by my own friends.

IZZY
You wouldn't have liked it anyway,

BECKS
Yeah! Sticky clubs,

FLO
Littered beaches,

IZZY
Unsanitary bathroom situations...

Again, the girls look to Fi to back them up.

FI
Well, um you wouldn't get your tits out I imagine?

KAT

You know what, I'm just going to, (moves to leave), I just need to check on the food in the kitchen,

BECKS

Didn't we order pizza?

IZZY

You're not upset are you? This was your idea. Your game. Your rules.

KAT

(a noticeable shift in temperament) You know what, yes, you're right. Why don't I read the rest of Becks'.

FI

I thought we were going one by one?

KAT

Who needs order? To hell with the rules!

FLO

But Kat,-

KAT

"Becks needs to stop with the lip filler and botox before she ends up looking like Katy Price."

BECKS touches her lips insecurely.

KAT (cont.)
Yeah sorry Becks, some, of the lads have started calling you "Special Effects Becks" – that's not on the card, I just thought I'd give you that one for free.
And last one,

FLO
Kat this is getting a little,-

KAT
"Becks should give up trying to be an influencer. It's not working and to be honest, is a bit embarrassing."
There. How does that feel?

BECKS
(visibly upset) Do all of you think this?

FLO
Becks, your influencer journey is just,-

KAT
Yes Becks, we all think this.
It's a superficial waste of your time and talents.
You're not a Kardashian for God's sake. Get a real job.

BECKS
Why are you being so mean?

BECKS leaves to go to the bathroom crying, exiting stage left. Bursts of sobbing will be heard sporadically throughout the rest of the scene.

FI

Kat, what the hell.

KAT

What? She'll get over it. It's good for her to know.
She'll probably even use this for content.

FI

Is this what you wanted? People crying,

KAT

What, you wrote that last one didn't you?
Come on, I know it was your handwriting.

IZZY

Kat this was all supposed to be anonymous!

FLO

You know, the new vibe in this room,
it's not good for my chakras.
I think I'll have to remove myself to protect my aura.

KAT

Perfect, go polish your rocks and tarot cards.

FLO

I know these words of anger are coming
from a place of hurt. I forgive you.

KAT

"Groovy", and the next time I see you
at the chicken shop I'll forgive you for

betraying your new 'vegan lifestyle'.

IZZY
Woah.

FLO is visibly offended and exits upstage right.

FI
This is all a bit intense. I'm going to check on Becks.

KAT
Don't you want to know your worst bits?

KAT snatches the cards off Izzy.

IZZY
Hey!

KAT
(reading)
"Fi would be better off if she stopped using casual sex as a means of distraction from her commitment issues." That's basically a nice way of saying you've never had a meaningful romantic relationship, probably because you won't let anyone love you since your mum left as a child.

IZZY
Oh my god, Kat.

KAT

And, last but not least "FI thinks she is smarter than all of us but actually she got the lowest marks in third year, we just didn't tell her. "

FI is taken aback.

KAT (cont.)

What? No witty retort?

FI

I'm going to check on Becks.

FI exits stage left.

KAT

(calling after FI) Hurts being lied to doesn't it!

Just IZZY and KAT left in the room.

IZZY

Kat, what's gotten into you? You're turning into a psycho bitch!

KAT

Better than a no-fun control freak isn't it? You know, I think I like anarchy.

IZZY

You've upset everyone!

KAT

Not everyone!...

KAT picks up the cards that BECKS has left behind.

KAT (cont.)

Don't you want to know what people said about you?

IZZY

Not really.

KAT

Ah, this is a good one: "Izzy gets so drunk when we go out that sometimes, I make sure to leave slightly early so I'm not stuck looking after her."
The drinking again, that's two-for-two
for you as well isn't it?

IZZY

Fine.

KAT

Isn't it *embarrassing* Iz?
Everyone basically thinks you're a boozy liability.

IZZY

Better than a pole-up-the-arse fun-spoiling,...
fun-spoiling-

KAT

What? Hangover got your words in a twist!

IZZY

Kat, you're just,-

KAT

Well while you're thinking of something to say,
I'll read you the one I wrote for you. "Izzy would –"

IZZY

(Quickly interrupts her, picking up FLO's cards)
"Kat, should know Arun has cheated on her with someone in this room."

Pause.
FLO enters. Shortly followed by FI and BECKS.

FLO

I forgot my lucky scarf.

FI

I think we're gonna head.

BECKS

Yeah, I don't feel so great.

Pause. Door bell rings.

KAT

Huh. Pizza's here.

IZZY

You know what, I'm not hungry.

BLACKOUT